# ALEXANDER GRAHAM BELL

## Inventor *of the* Telephone

*By the Editors of* TIME For Kids
WITH JOHN MICKLOS, JR.

HarperCollins*Publishers*

**About the Author:** John Micklos, Jr., is an award-winning educational journalist. He has written biographies and edited a series of children's poetry anthologies. A resident of Newark, Delaware, he enjoys working with students, helping them to cultivate a love of writing.

Library of Congress Cataloging-in-Publication Data is available.
ISBN-10: 0-06-057618-9 (pbk.) — ISBN-10: 0-06-057619-7 (trade)
ISBN-13: 978-0-06-057618-9 (pbk.) — ISBN-13: 978-0-06-057619-6 (trade)

1 2 3 4 5 6 7 8 9 10
First Edition

**Photography and Illustration Credits:**
Cover: Gilbert H. Grosvenor Collection–Library of Congress; cover inset: The Granger Collection–New York; cover flap: Library of Congress Prints & Photographs Division; title page: Parks Canada–Alexander Graham Bell National Historic Site of Canada; contents page: Gilbert H. Grosvenor Collection–Library of Congress; p.iv: Corbis; p.2: Mansell–Time Life Pictures–Getty Images; p.3: David E. Scherman–Time Life Pictures–Getty Images; p.4: Parks Canada–Alexander Graham Bell National Historic Site of Canada; p.5 (top): Parks Canada–Alexander Graham Bell National Historic Site of Canada; p.5 (bottom): Gilbert H. Grosvenor Collection–Library of Congress; p.6: Gilbert H. Grosvenor Collection–Library of Congress; p.7: Brown Brothers; p.8: The Alexander Graham Bell Family Papers–Library of Congress; p.9: Hulton-Deutsch Collection–Corbis; p.10–11: Bettmann–Corbis; p.11: Parks Canada–Alexander Graham Bell National Historic Site of Canada; p.12: Alexander Graham Bell Family Papers–Library of Congress; p.13 (top): Mansell–Time Life Pictures–Getty Images; p.13 (bottom): Parks Canada–Alexander Graham Bell National Historic Site of Canada; p.14 (top): Bettmann–Corbis; p.14 (bottom): Bettmann–Corbis; p.15: Science Museum–Science & Society Picture Library; p.16: National Railway Museum–Science & Society Picture Library; p.17: Bettmann–Corbis; p.18: Parks Canada–Alexander Graham Bell National Historic Site of Canada; p.19: Parks Canada–Alexander Graham Bell National Historic Site of Canada; p.20: Parks Canada–Alexander Graham Bell National Historic Site of Canada; p.21: The Granger Collection–New York; p.24: Chris Hellier/Corbis; pp.24–25: Library of Congress Prints & Photographs Division; p.25: Library of Congress Prints & Photographs Division; p.26 (top): Gilbert H. Grosvenor Collection–Library of Congress; p.26 (bottom): Mansell–Time Life Pictures–Getty Images; p.27: Minnesota Historical Society–Corbis; p.28: The Granger Collection–New York; p.29: Alexander Graham Bell Family Papers–Library of Congress; p.30: Gilbert H. Grosvenor Collection–Library of Congress; p.31 (top): The Granger Collection–New York; p.31 (bottom): Parks Canada–Alexander Graham Bell National Historic Site of Canada; pp.32–33: Gilbert H. Grosvenor Collection–Library of Congress; p.33: Parks Canada–Alexander Graham Bell National Historic Site of Canada; p.34: Courtesy National Geographic; pp.34–35: Brown Brothers; p.35: NASM–Smithsonian Images; p.36: Pix Inc.–Time Life Pictures–Getty Images; p.37: Bettmann–Corbis; pp.38–39: Mansell–Time Life Pictures–Getty Images; p.40: Corbis–PunchStock; p.41: Gilbert H. Grosvenor Collection–Library of Congress; p.42: Microsoft; p.43 (top): Loren Santow–Stone–Getty Images; p.43 (bottom): Stockdisc/Getty Images; p.44 (from top): AP, Robert B. Honeyman, Jr. Collection of early Californian and Western American Pictorial Material–Library of Congress, Corbis, The Granger Collection–New York; back cover: Mansell–Time Life Pictures–Getty Images

**Acknowledgments:**
For TIME FOR KIDS: Editorial Director: Keith Garton; Editor: Jonathan Rosenbloom; Art Director: Rachel Smith; Photography Editor: Bettina Stammen

 Find out more at **www.timeforkids.com/bio/bell**

# Contents

▲ **ALEXANDER GRAHAM BELL** holds a version of his telephone. His assistant, Thomas Watson, looks on.

## CHAPTER 1

# The Telephone Is Born

On March 10, 1876, Alexander Graham Bell toiled in his lab in Boston, Massachusetts. The lab was actually a few small bedrooms in a boardinghouse. Hanging on one of the walls was a portrait of an owl. It was given to the inventor as a joke because he often worked late into the night.

A pale, tall man with sideburns and a bushy mustache, Bell stared at his unusual contraption. He had been working on it for several years. Along the way, his invention had become an instrument of metal, rods, and wires.

> *"When one door closes another door opens; but we so often look so long and so regretfully upon the closed door, that we do not see the ones which open for us."*
>
> —ALEXANDER GRAHAM BELL

Bell had experimented with many other machines, but those trials had ended in failure. Sometimes he got discouraged, but he never gave up. Now history was about to be made.

To see if the device would work, Bell called into the mouthpiece: "Mr. Watson—Come here—I want to see you." Seconds later, his assistant burst through the door. He had heard Bell's voice, even though he was in another room with a hallway in between.

The two men switched places. Thomas Watson read from a book. A few of his words came through clearly. Then he said: "Mr. Bell, do you understand what I say?" Alexander Graham Bell heard every word.

◄ BELL'S FIRST telephone dates back to 1875. This is what his early model looked like.

THIS MODEL OF BELL'S FIRST TELEPHONE IS A DUPLICATE OF THE INSTRUMENT THROUGH WHICH SPEECH SOUNDS WERE FIRST TRANSMITTED ELECTRICALLY, 1875.

▲ YEARS after the telephone was invented, a couple has some fun with an early model.

After years of research, the telephone was finally born. Bell had built a machine that turned words into electric impulses. These impulses could be sent through a wire and heard at the other end.

Alexander Graham Bell's incredible invention was just the first step toward the modern telephone—a device that changed the world. Yet the real story of the telephone began many years before. It began when a young, curious boy tinkered with inventions in his parents' home. He was growing interested in a subject that had fascinated the Bell family for years—the science of speech.

## CHAPTER 2

# A Natural Inventor

lexander Bell was born on March 3, 1847, in Edinburgh, Scotland. (He added "Graham" to his name when he was a boy.) Aleck had an older brother, Melville (or "Melly"). He also had a younger brother, Edward, who was called Ted.

Aleck grew up in the perfect family for someone who

would later invent the telephone. His father, Alexander Melville Bell, was a well-known teacher and inventor who experimented with language and sound.

From an early age, Aleck shared his father's interest in

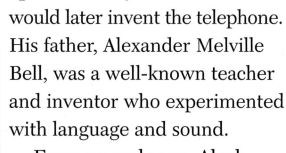

◄ ALECK'S FATHER, Alexander Melville Bell, was a teacher and inventor who inspired his son.

speech. He also wanted to know how things worked. One day Aleck's father said his watch needed cleaning. Trying to be helpful, Aleck took it apart. Then he cleaned it carefully—using a brush and soap and water. That was the end of the watch, but not the end of Aleck's curiosity.

Aleck's mother, Eliza Bell, became almost totally deaf when Aleck was ten. He was the only person she could understand without her hearing tube. Aleck had a special way of speaking to his mother. He would put his lips near her forehead and then speak in a low, clear voice.

Eliza was a talented artist and piano player. Aleck liked the piano, too. As a boy he could play pieces by heart. Eliza would press her hearing tube against the piano as he played. That way she could hear the music.

▲ IN 1855 ALECK'S FAMILY posed for this picture. From left to right, Melly, Aleck, Eliza, Ted, and Alexander.

Aleck made his first invention when he was about eleven years old. A friend's father owned a mill where Aleck and his friend often got into mischief. One day the owner told the boys to go do something useful. Aleck started making a machine that removed the husks from grains of wheat. His invention was used in the mill for a while, since it was so effective.

Aleck graduated from high school when he was thirteen years old. His parents sent him to London, England, when he was fifteen, to live and study with his grandfather, Alexander Bell. He was an actor who wrote books to help people speak better. During that year, Aleck changed from a shy boy to a confident young man.

# Studying Speech

In London Aleck met a man who used a machine to help him "speak." It produced only a few mechanical words, but it sparked Aleck's interest.

After Aleck returned to Scotland, his father challenged him and Melly to make their own speaking machine. So the boys designed a "talking skull." It took them two months to complete. They often thought of giving up, but they kept trying. Aleck worked this way all his life. If one way didn't work, he'd try another.

For the talking skull, Melly made the lungs, throat, and larynx. Aleck used wire and rubber to make the jaws, teeth, lips, and mouth. Melly blew air into the mouth through a tube. Then Aleck moved the mouth so sounds would come out. The boys made the machine cry "Mama!" The invention worked so well that a worried neighbor came to check on the crying baby!

Aleck got a job teaching music and speech at the Weston House Academy in 1863. At sixteen he was younger than some of his

▶ ALECK WAS VERY MATURE. He started teaching at age sixteen.

pupils, but he looked and acted several years older. Aleck loved teaching. From then on he tried to balance teaching and inventing.

Aleck spent the summer of 1865 studying Visible Speech, a system that his father created. It used thirty-four symbols to show every sound a human mouth could make. Aleck helped out his father at lectures. While Aleck was outside the room, audience members would suggest words. Aleck's father would write them in Visible Speech symbols. Aleck then went onstage, looked at the symbols, and pronounced the words. He was always right, even when the words were difficult!

Aleck and his father thought this system could be used to teach the deaf to speak. At the time, deaf children couldn't go to school with kids who could hear. Deaf adults had trouble getting jobs

ILLUSTRATIONS or VISIBLE SPEECH.

◀ VISIBLE SPEECH was a system of thirty-four symbols that stood for human sounds.

because their condition was so little understood. The Bells believed that the deaf would have better lives if they learned speech.

In 1865 the Bells moved to London. Aleck spent the next few years studying and teaching there. He worked with deaf children at one school. After giving a few lessons using Visible Speech, Aleck taught the children to speak words.

Because of his mother, Aleck knew how hard the world was for deaf people. Now he could help them.

Aleck had fun with projects like Visible Speech. They were serious attempts to learn more about the science of speech. Those experiments paved the way for his later work on the telephone.

## *The Industrial* REVOLUTION

**B**y the time Aleck was born in 1847, the Industrial Revolution was under way in Britain. The invention of different kinds of steam engines helped change the way goods were produced. They were once made by simple machines powered by water, wind, or wood. Now products could be made quickly and more efficiently.

These new machines and other inventions changed the way people lived. People flocked to the cities, where they began working in factories. They no longer stayed in the country and farmed their land. Soon the Industrial Revolution spread to the United States and other countries. It greatly influenced how we still live and work today.

## CHAPTER 3

# Life in the New World

The next few years were sad and difficult for the Bell family. Both of Aleck's brothers died of lung disease. Aleck himself often felt ill. He suffered from headaches, and he had trouble sleeping. His parents believed that the dirty air of big cities like Edinburgh and London had partly caused their sons' deaths.

In the summer of 1870, the Bells sailed from Europe for a new life in Canada.

▶ **THE HEAVY POLLUTION** in Edinburgh was one reason the Bells decided to move away.

They moved to a country home in Brantford, Ontario. The clear, crisp air soon made Aleck feel healthier, but it took him a long time to get over his brothers' deaths. Little by little he returned to doing what he loved best—teaching and learning about speech. Aleck even went to a nearby American Indian

village to record some Mohawk words in Visible Speech. While he was there, he learned a war dance. Sometimes, later in life, he did this dance when he got excited!

From time to time, Aleck and his father went to Massachusetts to give talks about Visible Speech. Sarah

▲ STUDENTS FROM Boston's Pemberton Avenue School for the Deaf pose for the camera. Aleck, on the top step on the right, taught at the school.

Fuller, the principal at the Boston School for Deaf Mutes, went to one of their lectures. Her school was the first-ever day school for the deaf. In 1871 she convinced the Boston School Board to hire Aleck to train the teachers in Visible Speech.

Aleck moved to Massachusetts to take on his new job and also to teach deaf children in schools. Within days he had made such progress with his students that a reporter from the *Boston Journal* wrote an article about him. Later that year he took on some deaf

children as private students,
helping them learn to speak.

When Aleck was twenty-six,
he became a professor at
Boston University, teaching
college students about speech.
He hoped to one day set up his
own school to instruct others to teach
the deaf. Aleck continued working with his private
students. One of them was a pretty teenage girl named
Mabel Hubbard. Little did the two young people
know what the future held for them.

Another private student was a
five-year-old boy named George
Sanders. His father, Thomas,
was very grateful to Aleck for
helping the boy learn to speak.
Thomas Sanders offered to pay
all of the young inventor's
expenses to do experiments
and, if anything should work
out, apply for patents.

Aleck was eager to experiment. He was now interested in the telegraph.

Invented in 1844 by Samuel Morse, this device allowed messages to be carried across long distances over wires. A person at one end of the line keyed in a message using a special code of dots and dashes. At the other end, someone else translated the code back into words. The telegraph made doing business much easier. But all messages had to be hand delivered from the telegraph station to the person receiving the message. And only one message could be sent over one wire at a time.

► THE MORSE RECEIVER made it possible to send messages cross-country.

Aleck wanted to improve the telegraph. He developed the harmonic telegraph. Since it used different pitches, many messages could be sent over the same wire at the same time. Each message would have its own sound.

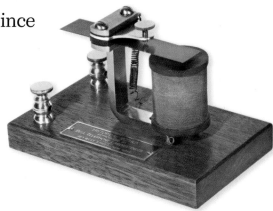

▼ THE HARMONIC TELEGRAPH was an improvement of Morse's machine.

## Patent Pending

Excited by the possibilities of the harmonic telegraph, Aleck planned to file a caveat with the United States Patent Office. (This is the government agency that registers inventions.) In a caveat inventors describe an idea for a new machine and declare that they will apply for a patent within three months. Caveats are a way to protect an idea from being stolen by others before an official patent can be filed.

Aleck spent the summer of 1874 in Brantford with his parents. For days on end he experimented with ways to send speech over a wire. He believed that sound waves could create an electrical current that would make it possible to do this. After all, if dots and dashes could travel over wires, why not voices? Slowly but surely Aleck was coming closer to his greatest invention.

# CHAPTER 4

# The Race for the Telephone

On his many visits to Mabel's home, Aleck would play the piano for the Hubbard family. One fall evening in 1874, Aleck told Mabel's father his idea for the harmonic telegraph.

Gardiner G. Hubbard thought it sounded like a moneymaker. He and Thomas Sanders became Aleck's partners. They provided money while Aleck provided ideas. About this same time Aleck was visiting a machine shop,

▶ ALECK MET his assistant in a machine shop like this one.

▲ THOMAS WATSON helped Aleck in the Boston lab. The two men worked long into the night on Bell's inventions.

where he met Thomas Watson. This young mechanic would work with Aleck for the next seven years. He would play a key role in helping Aleck with his inventions. Aleck kept working to perfect his harmonic telegraph. He also kept working on sending speech over a wire from one point to another.

Aleck applied for three patents. Each had to do with the telegraph. The Patent Office approved one, but the other two were held up for more study. At almost the same time, another inventor, Elisha Gray, had filed similar patents. The United States Patent Office had to decide who had thought of the ideas first.

## Sending Sounds

Aleck knew Elisha was competing with him on telegraph inventions. Soon they would also be racing to invent an "electrical speech machine." This machine would later be called the telephone.

By May 1875 Aleck knew he was on the edge of a major breakthrough. For months he worked feverishly on both the harmonic telegraph and the telephone, while still teaching. On June 2, 1875, Aleck was trying to transmit tones from one room to another over a wire. When Thomas Watson happened to pluck one of his receiver reeds, the reed in Aleck's room also vibrated. Thomas tried again. As he plucked the two reeds in his room, the reeds in Aleck's room both vibrated and made sounds. Aleck grew excited. This proved sounds could travel over wires. A month later Thomas heard Aleck's voice come through the telephone. But he couldn't make out any words.

Aleck was as determined in his love life as he was with his inventions. In June he realized he had fallen in love with Mabel. She was bright, lively, and caring. At first Mabel thought Aleck was a bit odd. But he would not give up. He wrote her letters. He visited her often. Over the next few months, his kindness won her over. On Thanksgiving Day, 1875, Aleck and Mabel became engaged. She soon persuaded him to drop the "k" from his name. He was now Alec.

▲ ALECK LOVED MABEL. After several months she realized she loved him too.

Alec's busy social life and stressful work life took its toll on him. He was having so many great experiences, yet he feared his inventions would not succeed. Exhausted and ill, he pushed himself by working late into the night.

Alec had written a patent description about the telephone in October 1875. Then he made a decision that nearly cost him his place in history. He wanted to apply for a patent in England before filing a patent in the United States. The patent office in London, however, showed no interest in the invention.

Alec finally filed his American patent on February 14, 1876. Just a few hours later that day, Elisha Gray filed a caveat explaining his idea for a telephone.

Only one of the men could get the patent. When Alec met with a patent official, he tried to prove that he had thought up important parts of the invention before Gray did. Whom would the official believe— Elisha or Alec?

◄ IT'S OFFICIAL! This letter says that Alec's patent was approved.

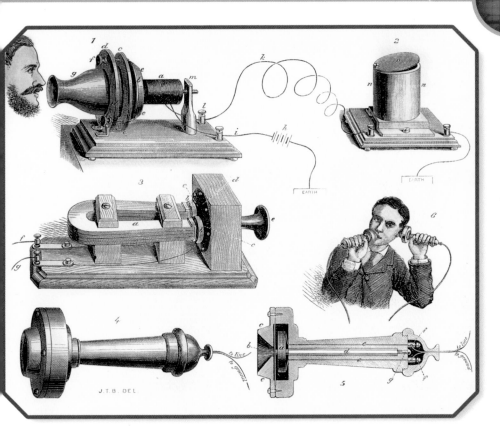

▲ PATENT 174,465 was issued on March 7, 1876. The drawing shows telephone parts.

On March 3, Alec's twenty-ninth birthday, the United States Patent Office sent him an official letter informing him that he would be receiving the patent for his telephone. Patent 174,465 was issued on March 7. It became one of the most valuable and important patents in history.

Just three days later, Alec and Thomas had their historic exchange. Alec didn't know it at the time, but his simple words, "Mr. Watson—Come here—I want to see you," would become world famous. And so would Alec.

## CHAPTER 5

# Building a Business

For several months few people were aware of the new invention. Then, in June 1876, Alec introduced the telephone at the Centennial Exhibition, a fair held in Philadelphia, Pennsylvania. He showed his invention to visitors from around the world. The instrument amazed everyone who saw it. An important guest at the fair, the emperor of Brazil, picked up the phone and heard Alec's voice on the other end. The emperor dropped the machine, saying, "My God, it talks!" Alec won a medal for his invention. Soon word about the telephone began to spread.

Alec was an inventor, not a businessman. He and his partners struggled at first. In fact, Gardiner Hubbard

▶ PEDRO II, THE EMPEROR OF BRAZIL, tried out Alec's telephone invention at the 1876 Centennial Exhibition in Philadelphia, Pennsylvania. Alec showed him how it worked.

offered to sell the rights for the telephone to the Western Union telegraph company for $100,000. Western Union refused. What a mistake! Later those rights proved to be worth hundreds of millions of dollars.

## A Rocky Start

The three partners formed the Bell Telephone Company in July 1877 to build and rent phones. But times continued to be hard for the new company. Fewer than a thousand Bell phones were in service after a few months. And phones could only be used to

call people in the same town. It didn't help when Western Union became a rival. Working with Elisha Gray and a young inventor named Thomas Edison, Western Union soon had telephones that worked as well as Bell's.

# Meet Me at THE FAIR

In 1876 Philadelphia, Pennsylvania, celebrated the one-hundredth birthday of the United States with a world's fair. It was popularly called the Philadelphia Fair or the Centennial Exhibition.

Visitors got to admire thousands of displays from thirty-seven nations. The event introduced people to different cultures and displayed the best products from many countries. But mostly it showed off how far the U.S. had come with its inventions and its industry.

Besides Bell's telephone, visitors could see the first typewriter and Edison's Electric Pen and Duplicating Press. They

▼ THE FAIR was open for only six months, but nearly nine million people visited it.

Bell Telephone was also at a disadvantage. Every time the company entered a new town, it had to build an expensive wiring system. Western Union simply used the wiring it already had in place, thanks to its telegraph business. It seemed as though Alec's new company might not survive.

Besides starting a new business in 1877, Alec also started a family. He married Mabel on July 11 at the Hubbards' home. One month later they sailed for Europe. Their voyage was part honeymoon and part business trip. They toured and had a

could also check out the giant Corliss Steam Engine, which was almost seventy feet tall and produced 1,400 units of horsepower.

Other exhibits showed different views of American life. One display included a model of a New England cottage. Another display with tepees and buckskin gave visitors an inside look at the life of American Indians. These were just a few of the many wonders at the fair.

▲ THE TORCH from the Statue of Liberty was on display at the Philadelphia Centennial Exhibition.

wonderful time. Alec relaxed for the first time in years. The Bells stayed for a few months in London, where Elsie was born in May 1878.

With growing fame and a contented family life, Alec was a happy man. Still, though he slowed his pace, he didn't stop working. Alec proudly demonstrated the telephone in England and France. He hoped people there would put money into his company.

## A Telephone Trial

When the Bells returned from Europe in the fall of 1878, Alec found himself swept up in business matters. Bell Telephone was suing Western Union.

The lawsuit said that because Alec had invented the telephone, his company should hold the only rights to sell it. Western Union didn't agree. It said that Elisha Gray had just as much right to the patent as Alec and his company did.

In 1879 a long court case began. It reached the highest court in the United States. The United States Supreme Court ruled that, until 1893, only Bell's company could sell telephones. Alec was about to become a very rich man.

─────────────────────

◄ ALEC GREW RICH from his invention. He even demonstrated his phone in England and France.

## CHAPTER 6

# Exploring More Ideas

In 1880 the French government awarded Alec the Volta Prize for his work on the telephone. He received about $10,000, which was a lot of money back then. Alec used the prize money to set up the Volta Laboratory in Washington, D.C. The Bells had been renting a home there. Later, as the Bells grew wealthier from the telephone, they were able to build a mansion. Though it brought him wealth and public appreciation, Alec disliked being

◀ MUSIC TO OUR EARS! Alec improved Thomas Edison's phonograph.

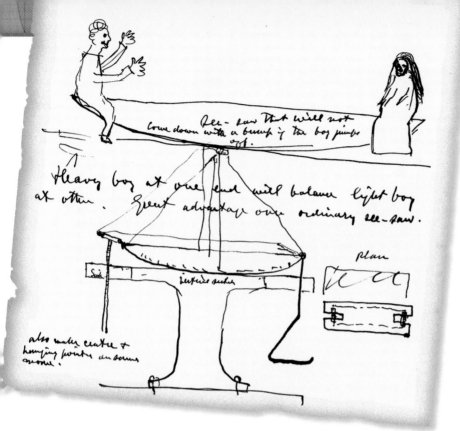

Bee-saw that will not come down with a bump if the boy jumps off.

Heavy boy at one end will balance light boy at other. Great advantage over ordinary see-saw.

plan

also under centre & hanging points in some

▲ ONE OF BELL'S IDEAS was to improve the seesaw. This is his sketch of it.

thought of only as the inventor of the telephone. The Volta Laboratory was also the site of endless other inventive ideas. One was an improvement of Thomas Edison's phonograph. Edison had invented a device that could play back recorded sounds. Alec made it work better.

The photophone was another idea that started in the Volta Laboratory. Using mirrors, sunlight, and a phone transmitter, Alec sent his voice through the air without wires. He also transmitted recorded music this way.

Alec was very excited by the idea of using natural sunlight to power a machine. Unfortunately the

machine wasn't practical. It didn't work well on cloudy days. It couldn't send sounds over long distances. But the photophone was just an invention ahead of its time. It came more than ten years before the radio, which also transmits sound without wires.

Alec liked the invention so much that when his second daughter was born in 1880, he wanted to name her Photophone. Mabel talked him out of it. The baby was named Marian and nicknamed Daisy.

## Trying to Save Lives

The Bells shared tragedy as well as happiness. In 1881 the Bells were looking forward to the birth of their third child. But the baby boy, whom they named Edward, died after just a few hours. Alec hoped to save

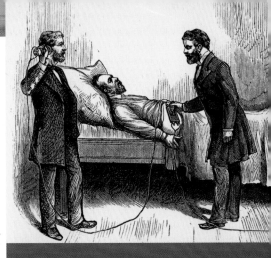

the lives of other babies like Edward. So he created a jacket that helped people who couldn't breathe on their own. It was an early version of the iron lung, a machine that saved thousands of lives in the twentieth century.

As always, Alec was coming up with inventions that helped to save lives and make life better for everyone.

## Trying to Save the
# PRESIDENT

In July 1881 President James Garfield was shot. A bullet lodged in his back. Alec had made a machine that could detect metal in the human body. Twice he took his invention to the White House and tried to find the bullet. Twice he failed.

Alec then developed a new type of probe. By this time, though, Garfield was much weaker. His doctors chose not to try the device.

President Garfield died on September 19, 1881. Alec's bullet probe didn't save him. But doctors still used his device until the early 1900s, when the X-ray became common and replaced the probe.

▲ **THE PHOTOPHONE** did not work over long distances, so it was never put into final production.

## CHAPTER 7

# Giving Back

**A**lec didn't spend all his life in a lab. The Bells sometimes traveled to Nova Scotia, Canada, a province by the Atlantic Ocean. There Alec fell in love with the land because it reminded him of Scotland. (Nova Scotia means "New Scotland.") Soon the family built a house near the shores of Baddeck Bay on Cape Breton Island. They called their property Beinn

► ALEC LOVED NATURE and animals. He raised sheep at his farm in Nova Scotia.

Bhreagh. This means "beautiful mountain" in Gaelic, an ancient language that is still spoken by some people in Scotland and Ireland. Over the years Alec did much of his research in Beinn Bhreagh.

Alec loved nature and animals. He raised and studied sheep in Nova Scotia. In 1888, at age forty, he became one of the first members of the National

▼ NOVA SCOTIA'S lovely coastline reminded Alec of Scotland.

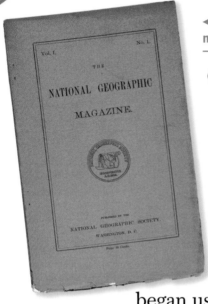

Geographic Society, which celebrated the outdoors. Alec helped start the famous *National Geographic* magazine. He even wrote articles for it, using the name H. A. Largelamb. When his secret was discovered, he began using his real name.

In 1898 the United States Congress made Alec a regent, or leader, of the Smithsonian Institution. (The Smithsonian is the national museum of the United States.) Alec helped the museum purchase a famous collection of Asian and American art, which visitors can still see today.

► VISITORS to Washington, D.C., can see the original building that was home to the Smithsonian Institution.

## Up and Away

Alec was restless for new areas to explore. With the Wright brothers' invention of the airplane in 1903, there seemed nowhere to go but up. Alec became an aviation pioneer. He helped to form a company called the Aerial Experiment Association. It built both kites and motor-powered airplanes. One of the group's most successful planes was the *Silver Dart*. On March 10,

1909, it flew in a circle over a distance of twenty miles. A few months later, the plane made the first passenger airplane flight in Canada.

# Mystery PERSON

**CLUE 1:** I was born in Tuscumbia, Alabama, in 1880. From a young age, I was deaf and blind.

**CLUE 2:** I met Alec when I was six years old. Alec helped my parents find me a teacher, Anne Sullivan. She taught me to communicate with the world around me.

**CLUE 3:** I became a famous writer and speaker. My book, *The Story of My Life,* is dedicated to Alec.

Who am I?

ANSWER: HELEN KELLER

Alec also developed a hydrofoil. This was a boat built on pontoons, which look similar to skis. Powered by propellers, it skimmed over the top of the water. In 1919 one model reached a speed of seventy-one miles per hour. This set a world record that wasn't broken for over ten years.

## Support the Deaf

Above all else, Alec thought of himself as a "teacher of the deaf." The Volta Laboratory was turned into a center of information on deafness. He started what is now known as the Alexander Graham Bell Association for the Deaf and Hard of Hearing. The group still exists today.

▲ **ALEC NEVER GAVE UP** teaching deaf people to communicate.

Many people changed their opinions about the deaf, thanks to Bell's work. In 1918 the city of Chicago built a new school. Deaf and hearing children still had separate classes there, but they came together at recess. This made it possible for them to get to know one another. Alec had supported this idea for years. City leaders named the school after him. Alec took special pride in this honor. All his life his goal was to have deaf people treated with respect. He wanted them to work together with others and to build normal lives.

## CHAPTER 8

# A Wonderful Life

Alec was more forward thinking than most people of his time. He supported women's rights, especially their right to vote. He believed that people of all races should have equal rights. In the early 1900s Alec also wrote about the dangers of global warming. He came up with the phrase "greenhouse effect," a common term today.

As he had hoped, long-distance wires would connect phones in distant cities. By 1907 more than six million phones were in use. In 1915 Alec placed the first coast-to-coast call from New York City. Thomas Watson, his former assistant, was in San Francisco. Alec repeated the words from the first telephone call: "Mr. Watson—Come here—I want to see you." This time it would have taken Thomas a week to join Alec!

## A Favorite Place

Beinn Bhreagh became a favorite place for the Bells to spend time. As their daughters married and had families, the house filled up with children and grandchildren. Alec and Mabel set up a public library and a reading club for young women in a nearby village. Alec was happy. For perhaps the first time in his adult life, he relaxed.

▲ THE FIRST TRANSCONTINENTAL PHONE CALL was made from New York City in 1915. Alec (center) just finished calling San Francisco.

## Bells Are RINGING

The decibel is a unit used to measure the volume of sound. It is named after Alexander Graham Bell. Here are the decibel levels for some common sounds. Noises over 85 decibels can damage your hearing if you listen too long.

| | |
|---|---|
| 10 | breathing |
| 20-30 | soft whisper |
| 60 | normal conversation |
| 70-80 | vacuum cleaner |
| 70-90 | busy traffic |
| 90-100 | motorcycle |
| 110-120 | music at a rock concert |
| 120-150 | jet engine during takeoff |
| 180 | rocket launching from pad |

Colleges showered Alec with awards. He was even honored by the people in Edinburgh, the city where he was born.

As he aged, Alec's health began to fail. He was overweight. He also had diabetes and other serious health problems.

Yet Alec kept working on projects until his death. He passed away on August 2, 1922, holding Mabel's hand. Alec was buried on the mountaintop at Beinn Bhreagh. In his honor telephones across the United States fell silent for one minute.

In 1965, long after his death, Alexander Graham Bell was named to the Aviation Hall of Fame in Dayton, Ohio, for his work on kites and airplanes.

Bell became a very good businessman, but he did not think of himself that way. Instead he thought of himself as an inventor, a teacher of the deaf, and someone who wanted to make people's lives easier.

Alexander Graham Bell had been proud of what he had accomplished during his life. As an inventor he stuck with his ideas and never gave up. As a teacher he worked hard to help the deaf speak and to improve their education. Alexander Graham Bell made remarkable progress in the science of speech, which had fascinated him since he was a child. Thanks to his efforts, communications improved for all people all over the world.

# Talking About Alexander

▲ Bill Gates

TIME For Kids editor Kathryn Satterfield interviewed computer software creator Bill Gates about Alexander Graham Bell.

**Q:** *What does it take to be an inventor?*
**A:** It's important to have a deep curiosity about how things work, to read a lot, and to combine knowledge from many areas to come up with something new. It takes patience to keep experimenting and figuring out why things worked—and why they didn't—until you discover something truly magical.

**Q:** *How did Bell's work influence later inventions?*
**A:** Alexander Graham Bell's work on the telephone was very important in helping us understand

electricity and electronics—which helped bring about many inventions, including the computer. Bell also pioneered the idea of using electricity to carry information over long distances. The Internet as we know it certainly wouldn't exist without that insight.

**Q:** *How do you think inventing and helping young people are connected?*
**A:** Many great inventions have come from the curiosity of young minds. And the way children use technology has greatly influenced the way I think about where computers are going. So by investing in young people, we're investing in future generations of inventors.

# Alexander Graham Bell's
# KEY DATES

| | |
|---|---|
| **1847** | Born on March 3, in Edinburgh, Scotland |
| **1870** | Moves to Canada with his family |
| **1871** | Begins teaching deaf students in Boston, Massachusetts |
| **1876** | Invents the telephone |
| **1877** | Marries Mabel Hubbard |
| **1880** | Invents the photophone |
| **1888** | Becomes a founding member of the National Geographic Society |
| **1909** | Helps design an airplane, the *Silver Dart* |
| **1915** | Places the first coast-to-coast telephone call |
| **1922** | Dies on August 2, at Beinn Bhreagh in Canada |

**1850** California becomes the thirty-first state in the U.S.

**1885** Bicycle invented.

**1914** World War I begins.

jB        Alexander Graham
BELL      Bell.

$14.99

| DATE | | | |
|---|---|---|---|
| | | | |
| | | | |
| | | | |
| | | | |
| | | | |
| | | | |
| | | | |
| | | | |
| | | | |
| | | | |
| | | | |
| | | | |